Disclai

All rights reserved. No part of this book may be reproduced in any form without permission in writing from the author. Reviewers may quote brief passages in reviews.

No part of this publication may be reproduced or transmitted in any form or by any means, mechanical or electronic, including photocopying or recording, or by any information storage and retrieval system, or transmitted by email without permission in writing from the publisher.

While all attempts have been made to verify the information provided in this publication, neither the author nor the publisher assumes any responsibility for errors, omissions or contrary interpretations of the subject matter herein.

Neither the author nor the publisher assumes any responsibility or liability whatsoever on the behalf of the purchaser or the reader of these materials.

Table of Contents

Incipient Thoughts

Chapter 1: Managers' objectives

Chapter 2: Management vs. Leadership

Chapter 3: The philosophy of Leadership

Chapter 4: Why Managers Must be Leaders

Chapter 5: The Core Skills Needed for Managing Teams

The Essence of Delegation

The Importance of Motivation

Chapter 6: Developing Teams

The bottom line of developing people

The self-assessment process

The 360 feedback

Chapter 7: Improving Communication and Team Work

Learn to listen

Be aware of Other People's Emotions

Empathize

Encourage

Use Humor

Treat People Equally

Attempt to Solve Conflicts

Maintain a Positive Attitude and Smile

Minimize Stress

Chapter 8: Coaching Teams for Increasing Performance

Understand the Team Dynamics

The Main Barriers of Effective Group Dynamics

Set Behavioral Expectations

Support Individual Development

Chapter 9: The Model of Effective Management

Emotional competence

Conceptual competence

Technical competence

Integrity

Professionalism

Respect for diversity

Chapter 10: The Main Pillars of Emotional Competence

Chapter 11: The Main Pillars of Conceptual Competence

Chapter 12: The Main Pillars of Technical Competence

Continuous Learning and Development

Chapter 13: Emotional Intelligence: The Binder between Leadership and Management

Emotional Intelligence- Molder of the Leadership Process

Self-awareness in Leadership

Self-regulation- A Star Leader's Secret Weapon

Self-Motivation in Leadership

Empathy: The Force That Moves Business Forward

Social Skills in Leadership

Incipient Thoughts

The future of work environment depends on the manager's ability to be a good leader for his team(s).

They are placed in that position of power because they have earned followers, through leadership and respect, and through recognition of people's involvement in complying with the rules and objectives of the company.

There are managers who are very skilled at making strategic decisions. They are focused only on bringing profits to the company. They achieve it at the price of sacrificing people's salaries, time, and satisfaction.

They continue to do this as long as it works. But how long does it work? This type of management brings dissatisfaction for employees and leads to reduced productivity. They will stop working properly because there's no one to listen to their needs and their work expectations.

In business, people tend to focus more on the glamorous work of leadership that brings vision, inspiration, and challenge, and less on the implementation of efficient management.

A successful organization is the outcome of an efficient management, reflected in hard work, productive and effective workforce that punches above its weight in its performance, and efficacious communication.

Good managers attract exceptional employees for the organization, creating a strong bond between them and their teams, which are based on trust, commitment, and engagement.

The strong relationship between teams is not a happenstance, it is the result of an excellent management that inspires the followers in respecting the rules of the organization, working productively, and following the vision.

But following a vision when you can't understand its horizons is hard. You need to have someone to make it simple for you.

That's the role of the manager. They help teams understand their position in the organization and how their contribution leads to success.

Because, in the end, what's the meaning of the vision?

A big picture of what success will be in a particular moment in the future.

The vision encompasses the answers to many questions:

What does our organization look like?

How big is it?

What are we famous for?

Why does anyone care about what we do?

How do people who work here feel about their jobs?

What's my role in it?

The vision makes the process of handling strategic opportunities that arise every day simpler.

They are calls that come in every day and they are worth considering only if they follow the predetermined steps of the long-term view called vision.

The managers' responsibility consists in supporting their teams, driving highly effective projects, and getting the best performance from employees even in difficult and stressful situations and increasing workloads.

Being a good manager requires an extensive set of skills, from planning of activities and delegation of tasks to prompt communication skills and a powerful ability to motivate people.

The ability of understanding people might be an innate skill but you can also work on it to improve its potential.

The truth is that a strict management model is not enough to bring the organization to the highest level. The need of using the basic principles of leadership is necessary.

There are recognizable characteristics in great leaders and simple strategies to apply for improving the performance of employees and to change the work environment.

Because managers do things in the right way, while leaders are more concerned in doing the right things for organization and also for their teams.

Managers are more concerned in accomplishing big and promising projects and deadlines and this leaves little room for leadership activities.

This leads to dissatisfaction from employees, because they will believe that their needs are not important and no one listens to their problems.

This is one of the reasons for the unproductive work done by employees, because they are not motivated to improve their skills and abilities and compete to the new changes in the work environment and technology.

They will get the same benefits (recognition, money, bonuses) as the ones who work hard, but with less effort and involvement.

Employee need to know how their roles and responsibilities add value and lead the organization to success.

They need to be appreciated for their work and also warned when they do it wrong to improve their performance and find out where they underperform.

Chapter 1: How Managers Do Their Job

When it comes to understanding the manager's role in the organization, there are five big pillars established by Peter Drucker, one of the fathers of management, which define an effective management, seen also through the mirror of leadership:

Managers set objectives. They set the short- and long-term goals for organization, deciding the tasks for each day and delegating people to accomplish them. Their objectives follow the SMART criteria of setting goals: Specific, Measurable, Attainable, Realistic, Time-based.

Managers organize. They divide the work into manageable activities.

Managers measure performance. This means that they establish appropriate targets that need to be achieved and yardsticks for work, and ways of analyzing, appraising, and interpreting the performance of the work and employee.

Managers motivate and communicate. The manager creates a team out of his people, through decisions on pay, placement, promotion, and through his communications with the team. Communication plays a decisive role in understanding the psychology of the teams and how you can integrate people efficiently in the work environment, because integration has significant influence in the performance of the employee. Drucker also referred to this as the "integrating" function of the manager.

Managers develop people. As the business advances over time, the development of employees becomes an immense, fundamental, and necessary concern of managers, leaders, and employers. Why develop people?

Think about the advancement of technology, mobility, globalization, and behavioral changes.

For so many years, people were focused on a job and they have learned how to be efficient in doing the tasks linked to that job.

Then everything changes, the work environment changes.

Flexibility determines the rules of the workplace.

Employee have to learn more and do more tasks using the same amount of time and resources, but at the same time, do it the right way, using new technologies.

Most of them fail from lack of knowledge or resistance to changes.

The manager's duty is to coach people. Coaching is a useful way of developing people' skills and abilities, and of boosting performance.

It also helps people deal with issues and challenges before they turn into major problems.

Chapter 2: Management vs. Leadership

The two words are sometimes used interchangeably, but they don't represent the same mission.

But even those who represent these jobs are sometimes confused about the true meaning of management or leadership.

The truth is that not all leaders are managers and not all managers are leaders.

Leadership goes beyond the management system and process.

Management involves getting things done using the given resources, the patterns and rules within the organization, control of the work during the process, and determination of whether employees meet the expectations, whereas leadership is the capacity and act of creating compelling visions, translating them into actions, and sustaining them.

Leaders inspire people to believe in these visions and treat them as their own.

Management is about telling people what to do whereas leadership is about helping people to do what they have asked them to do.

I believe that leaders are the improved prototypes of managers.

They not only master the art of organizing things in a strict order, giving people the direction for achieving results, but they also continually thrive for the development of their people. They coach them for performance, they coach them to embrace the change as an opportunity to grow and expand the knowledge limits rather than perceiving the change as a headache, a new shift in the system, new rules to follow, and new operations to learn.

Managers set the budget of the projects and plan the process and organize the structure of the teams, whereas leadership is oriented toward bringing people with different backgrounds together and making them to work as an effective team- aligning them, motivating them to believe in the potential of their ideas, and mentoring them in their daily activities.

A distinct aspect seen as a key factor in increasing peoples' productivity is the ability of leaders to listen to peoples' needs.

A simple manager will not focus his attention on what motivates people to work harder and achieve greater results.

He will set the standards and control if they are followed and if the final result corresponds to the desired one.

What a leader does is coaching.

He coaches people to discover what kind of factors from their personal life inspires and motivates them to work for the organization's purposes.

He wants to find out how the peoples' purposes correspond to the organization's objectives.

If he manages to align the peoples' needs with the organization's purposes, then productivity will be definitely improved.

People are motivated to work when they have an inner impetus that stimulates them.

When they know that the leader will praise them for the work they do, they will be more stimulated to do that task. Leadership and management skills are not hereditary traits; they can be learned and developed.

Although managers can be appointed for their position and mission, leaders have to gain their position; they have to be elected by their team.

Even though the organization can't run without managers, the need of an inspiring leader can is more powerful. This is why managers should practice both management and leadership for fulfilling the company and employees' needs.

Chapter 3: The Philosophy of Leadership

The impact and influence leaders mostly desire is achieved through 6 practices*: **envision, enlist, embody, empower, evaluate, and encourage.***

1. They have ***a clear vision*** of the future and they are compelled by it, they want to work toward that vision. They have long-term dreams, and magnificent goals and expectations.

It is said that an organization without a vision perish.

2. Another practice of leadership is about ***enlisting.***

That's the moment when you encourage people to share ideas, needs, perspectives, their dreams, their desires from where you, the leader, can start shaping your vision.

People mostly support what they create. That happens when a leader calls people to bring input, to brainstorm, to envision, to see them involved in the process.

3. The third thing leaders do is to embody their vision.

This happens when there is a congruence between who they are and what they want to show to their people. If you want to be a leader who leads by example, well, you have to become an example.

As a leader, your words have to correspond to your behavior and actions.

Leaders have to stand for, demonstrate, and portray what they believe in.

They have to believe in their ideas even in bad conditions, when people don't believe, and when people give up.

4. The next practice is empowerment.

Leaders empower people, giving them the authority to make decisions and the trust that they will do the right things.

Leaders empower people to use their skills, tools, knowledge, equipment, and technology to work toward the vision and make it become real.

5. Evaluation is the hardest thing leaders do in their day-to-day activities.

They evaluate the people who work with them, their contribution, their skills, and the ethics are going on in the organization.

Is the team progressing?

Are we performing according to our expectations?

Are we being ethical?

Are we moving forward?

This is an excellent tool to give feedback to the team and the people who are influencing the performance of the organization.

6. The last practice and the one that makes the difference is encouraging people on a continuous basis.

A leader inspires and motivates people.

A leader has to motivate people with passion and example.

A leader has to deal with challenges, conflicts, turbulences, struggles, and frustration.

He has to direct people straight to the mission. He has to be constantly involved in the process and involve others, too.

People are collaborators; they don't follow you, they are engaged in the process.

Chapter 4: Why Managers Must be Leaders

This question must have entered your mind when you saw the title of the book.

The answer might be hidden in the substrate of the following quote: "Leaders are people who do the right things; managers are people who do things right."

The odds say that managers and leaders are two separate people who work within the organization, but this is a quite harmful assumption.

There are a lot of managers who don't know how to lead and a lot of leaders who cannot manage.

There are leaders who create enlightening visions but they don't know how to implement them and control the process of implementation.

There are managers who know how to enforce visions and verify the process, but they don't know how to involve people in the process, and build trust and engagement.

They don't know how to inspire people to believe in their ideas and take them for granted.

In the past, the role of the manager was to enforce control, making sure that people were showing up on time, doing their job, and don't cause problems. There was no interest in creativity, innovation, engagement, and empowerment. Or maybe, there was no need for them, which can be true if you analyze the main objectives of the old organizational concepts.

The modern organizational concepts are based on development, effectiveness, competitiveness, and the ability of coping with changes in society, mentality, and innovation.

In the background of development, which is followed by an activated and inspired organizational climate, leaders play a crucial role in promoting values, sharing information, amplifying outcomes, and innovating concepts for organizational prosperity and performance, empowering people to take attitude and express their ideas freely.

For leaders, each idea counts. But first, they have to make sure that those ideas are clearly pointed and everyone can understand them. From this comes another mission of leaders, the one of aligning different cognitions and values among organization concepts and expectations. They make teams understand different opinions and spread the information acquired in the organizational environment.

Leaders encourage people to come up with ideas, managers only implement them.

The organization vision stands in the competence of people to do the right things in the right way at the right time.

The stereotypical managers are concentrated on control, productivity, delegation of tasks, efficiency, the bottom line, and process whereas leaders are focused on visions, new ideas, changes, transformation, engagement, empowerment, and habit enhancements.

Leadership requires creating a spellbinding vision of the future, communicating that vision, and helping people to understand and commit to it.

Managers are responsible for ensuring that the vision is enforced effectively and successfully.

The overall effectiveness is provided by fulfilling both roles at the same time.

The biggest problem for companies today is that they are taking people from the positions of power and training them to be good leaders.

Why is that a problem? Because the ability of being a leader is innate, it comes from within. You have to believe and feel that you are meant to be a leader.

You can't be trained to be leader...Yes, you can be trained to become a manager.

Companies should discover people within the organization with leadership skills and train them to manage.

Managers must be leaders!

One without the other is meaningless!

Chapter 5: The Core Skills Needed for Managing Teams

Managers are the engine that drives companies to performance and effectiveness.

To accomplish their mission, they should have a certain range of skills.

The Essence of Delegation

Even "Super You" needs some help and support from time to time. In that moment, you need to leave your pride behind and let people show their abilities while working for the team goals.

"There is no such thing as a single-handed success; when you include and acknowledge all those in your corner, you propel yourself, your teammates, and your supporters to greater heights."

One of the greatest limitations we encounter in life is time. Our success depends on the time we allocate to being productive in our work. With so many tasks, how productive can we become?!

With limited resources, success is limited.

One of the most common ways of overcoming limitations is to learn how to delegate your work to other people.

Successful delegation brings a lot of benefits for managers and their teams. Managers have the opportunity to create strong teams and meet the demands, while employees can learn how to work in teams and bring input to achieve the team goals.

Why managers don't delegate:

- the fear of losing control of the projects
- the fear or dislike of employee taking credit or sharing the limelight
- they don't have time to train employees delegation techniques or supervise their work
- they worry that employees will commit huge mistakes or use methods they weren't allowed to use.

These are problems that managers can fix.

If your fear as a manager is that you will lose the control of your own work, remember that you have the power to check the progress of the work and require employees to check it with you, and that you can also set the schedule for the deadlines. If you delegate from the sense of your own power, your fears will definitely fade away.

If your fear is that an employee will take credit or share the limelight, remember that an important part of your role within the organization is to be a mentor. You have to guide them and take their failures as yours and their successes, too. Work hard to thrive for success, but don't discredit them if they fail. Just direct them to the right paths.

If one of your employees tries to take credit, you have the power to erase the expressions of ego or unjust competitiveness.

If you think you don't have time to delegate or supervise, remember that this is the managers' job.

And you don't have to be completely involved in the training for delegation. You need to give credit to people and support them in learning from experience. You have to encourage your teams to develop new skills, but you still have to control the process from the shadows.

If you worry about the mistakes your employee will make, remember that a significant part of the learning process is the ability to learn from your mistakes.

An important part of effective delegation strategy is the time you allow for planning, supervision, scheduling, and error correction.

There will be a lot of gains that will come to you as an effective delegator. You will have the opportunity to develop satisfied and productive employees who not only think for themselves but also view you as an effective mentor and supervisor, someone they can rely on and go for advice without the fear that their projects will be taken away from them or rejected. You will have more time for your innovative tasks that require a unique approach and expertise.

Another benefit of a successful delegation is the enhancement of your reputation, which leads to the possibility of advancement.

The Appropriate Time for Delegation

Delegation is a win-win process when it is done effectively. This is why you can't delegate tasks to everyone. You have to determine, based on a set of questions, the tasks you need to delegate and the right people who are skilled for completing them.

- Is there someone who has the necessary information or expertise to complete the tasks? Is that a task someone can do or is critical that you do that?

- Does the task provide the opportunity of developing someone's skills?

- Is this a task that will occur in the future, in a different form?

- Do you have enough time to delegate effectively? The process is based on training, setting goals, checking progress, and error correction.

- Is it a task you should delegate? You should delegate the tasks that require only short-term attention. The tasks that can affect the long-term performance of company should receive only the manager's attention.

The Main Principles of the Delegation Process

1. As a manager, you have to be very specific with the desired outcome.

2. Clearly identify boundaries and constraints. Determine the level of authority, accountability, and responsibility.

3. Involve more people in the delegation process and give them the liberty to choose what tasks are delegated to them and when.

4. Set the amount of responsibility with the amount of accountability.

5. Delegate tasks to the lowest possible organizational level. There are people who are more familiar with the tasks you're delegating or they are more acknowledged to do it. This will increase the performance and efficiency of the process.

6. Provide support to your team. Communicate effectively and monitor the process.

7. Focus on outcome. You should be concerned with the results of delegation rather than focusing your energy on describing how the work should be done. Your method is not the only one or the best one. Try to involve people in the process and give credit to them. Trust is one of the ways of getting people committed.

8. Build motivation and commitment. Discuss the opportunities, financial rewards, and recognition that accomplishing tasks will bring.

9. Establish and control regularly. Set objectives, discuss timelines and deadlines, make adjustments where necessary, and take time to verify the work at the end.

Keep Controlling and Give Feedback

Once you have established the necessary steps for accomplishing the delegated tasks, try to explain to your team why you have chosen them to do that task, what you are expecting from them, and the goals you have for the project. Set timelines, deadlines, and resources needed for it. Try to set a schedule for the meetings for checking the progress your team is making.

One of the most important things is to make sure your team knows that you want to be informed about changes or problems that occur during the process and also that you are open to help and guide them.

Another fundamental aspect: As a manager you shouldn't micromanage, but it doesn't mean that you have to give up all control. In effective delegation, the manager has the duty of monitoring and supporting closely enough to ensure that the tasks is done correctly and effectively, while giving enough space for people to come out with their abilities, skills, and strategies.

Why Give Full Acceptance?

After finishing the delegation process, take time to revise the work your team has finished. You have to accept only good quality, fully-completed work.

If you accept a project that is not completed or that you are not satisfied with, your team will not learn how to do the work better, because you haven't set higher goals and expectations. Plus, you have to get the work done by yourself.

If you are satisfied with the results you have received from your team, you have to recognize and reward the efforts and input.

Another aspect that really works for leaders is to compliment people every time you notice and you are impressed by someone's work.

This is the first step in building self-confidence and efficiency.

The Importance of Motivation

A paycheck is not enough to motivate employees. Maybe it was enough in the past, but now, an annoying boss, an uncomfortable work space, or an absurd set of rules will make people lose their interest in work productivity.

Ineffectively managed environmental factors lead to demotivating people and miserable behaviors. Even if they are

People are motivated by leaders they want to follow and tasks worth doing. But it is still not enough. There is a set of methods of helping people be productive and perform to the best of their ability.

1. **Support new ideas**. People come with ideas or solutions to problems because they are interested in helping; that's a sign that they care about their mission. Encouraging people to give input into the organization motivates them.

2. **Empower each individual**. Every single individual contributes to the achievement of the organization's goals. Empower them to bring value through their ideas. This creates a

sense of ownership that leads to exceeding personal and professional expectations.

3. **Listen to them**. It might seem very easy, but it turns out to be the most difficult thing sometimes. Not only does it make him feel that he is respected and someone cares about his problems, concerns, and ideas, but you can also get objective insight into the business you're managing.

4. **Reward accomplishments**. Do you know what makes people feel like they're in seventh heaven? The answer is "reward". Not money, even if that is the main purpose of their work, but the recognition for the accomplishments achieved, action taken, and attitudes exemplified through their behavior.

5. Another aspect is **appreciation**, which means expressing gratitude about the excellent performance of someone. Doing this in front of the team makes that person feel respected, appreciated, and it gives a sense of accountability and pride.

6. **Be a leader worth following.** If your employees don't perceive you as a leader, how can you convince them to work to accomplish your vision and mission?

7. **Encourage learning new skills.** The development of your employee should be one of the most important aspects. Times are changing and step by step, old skills become insufficient for achieving the competitive advantage.

8. **Create a career path.** This is one of the strongest motivators. Employees who have a path set before them that may lead to promotion can work towards a goal. It leads to increased commitment to accomplishing the company's goals.

9. **Create attainable goals.** Setting goals might be easy, but you have to determine if they can be accomplished by your team. Don't make people work in vain for a goal that can't be achieved on a specific time or can't be achieved at all.

10. **Encourage individuality.** Every individual is unique. Encouraging individual personalities will create a more dynamic and diverse culture within the organization.

11. **Give them a reason to come to work every day.** Try to lift the morale of your employees, because going to the same job every day turns into an exhausting routine. Try to free people from the routine. You should encourage them to switch tasks, provide them trainings on the topics they choose, or teambuilding.

Chapter 6: Developing Teams

Helping people to get on the verge of their performance

"The growth and development of people is the highest calling of leadership."

One of the appropriate moments for a manager to turn into a leader worth following is the moment when he has to develop people.

Most leaders believe that people are the most important assets and are all too conscious of the stubborn competition for talent and performance.

The bottom line of developing people:

1. Attract and retain highly effective and talented employees
2. Maximize performance
3. Communicate respect
4. Build trust and positive relationships
5. Establish a culture of abiding learning

Five steps that move you forward:

1. Own it!
2. Determine strengths and opportunities
3. Conduce a development conversation
4. Create a development plan
5. Monitor progress and provide feedback.

Step 1: Own it!

As a leader, you get most of the things done through others. A fundamental part of your responsibility is to magnify the performance of every person from your team.

This means to determine their strengths, uncover their hidden talents, discover weaknesses and turn them into powerful advantages, find possible opportunities, and unravel obstacles in the development process.

Starting a development conversation with your employee allows you to find new ways of enhancing performance from two different perspectives: employer and employee.

Getting answers to the right questions can unveil opportunities that can contribute to the personal and professional development of the employee and also obstacles that can reduce the clarity of the process.

Taking action toward this process is a sign of commitment to the development of your team and the lasting success of the company.

Step 2: Determine strengths and opportunities

It's important to gather information from different sources, such as employee feedback, team feedback about someone else's performance, or you can use self-assessments or 360-feedback process.

The self-assessment process can be implemented to determine a person's perception of the abilities he possesses because that perception of his abilities may significantly influence the actions he takes.

The saddest truth about people's abilities is that they underestimate them. Most of the time, they believe they don't have the required set of skills to succeed.

This is the moment when personal and professional development has a huge impact.

As a leader, if you determine the strengths someone has, you will be able to improve his image about himself. The result is a boost of self-confidence.

You will also discover the weak parts of someone's personality and you can improve them.

The self-assessment process:

On a self-assessment process, you should consider the following questions:

1. What is most satisfying, meaningful, or compelling about the current work you do?

2. What are your strengths? In what areas are you performing at the top of your performance?

3. What skills do you have that you are not currently using?

4. What is most challenging? What nags at you or keeps you up at night?

5. How do you think others perceive you?

6. What are areas to improve to move you to achieve performance?

7. What are the skills you want to develop?

8. What knowledge would you like to acquire?

9. What opportunities would provoke/challenge you?

The 360 feedback

The 360 feedback is an effective method of providing professional feedback through enabling coworkers to express their honest feedback about employee performance.

The name of the process comes from the fact that the performance feedback is required from all the directions of the organization.

The purpose of this type of review is to provide positive and constructive feedback. The manager wants to discover aspects that need to be improved and then he will design an improvement plan for each employee who needs development.

This type of method is effective when it is done correctly, when the managers and the employees engaged in the process are objective towards someone else's performance or deficiency, when their ideas are not influenced by antipathy, old misunderstanding, envy, the organizational level where the reviewer activates (whether is on a lower level or top level), and the way the reviewer perceives that person.

To improve employee performance, a leader should be focused on determining areas he needs to improve, like skills, abilities, or competencies someone lacks.

In this way, the leader will translate the organization/department mission into specific, achievable goals that the employee can understand and work for, manage someone's performance instead of reacting to it, get new ideas and information from staff, discuss skills and career development, reduce the stress of supervisors by managing them in an appropriate way, and reduce the stress of employees by making your expectations more clear.

Step 3: Conduce a development conversation

An efficient and beneficial development conversation is based on collaboration.

Firstly, you have to review the employee's self-assessment and the feedback you have gathered, then preparc your speech in a way you know that will influence positively the employee you're trying to develop.

At the beginning of the conversation, try to adjust the tone of your voice (hospitable, constructive, and friendly) and provide an overview of the performance of the employee. At the end, show your appreciation, confirm the next steps, and schedule a follow-up meeting in which you will examine the progress.

I will give you some of the most effective questions to discuss during the meeting with your employee:

1. Given your self-assessment, what goals will you set for yourself?

2. What resources will you need to accomplish these goals?

3. How and when will we jointly assess progress?

4. What do you need from me to be successful in accomplishing these goals?

5. What will you do to develop members of your team?

6. How do you prefer to be recognized or acknowledged for the work you do?

7. What role or position would you like to have three years from now?

How much of your time would you sacrifice to get there? (in terms of improving skills and abilities)

Step 4: Create a development plan

The next step is to ask your employee to create a development plan based on the goals, skills, strengths, opportunities, weaknesses, obstacles, actions, or evidence of success.

Provide him with the necessary guidelines, such as:

1. Ask him to choose few goals for improvement. Direct him to set those goals to solve a problem, to be specific. They should have significant meaning for him, should make a difference within the organization, and be within his control. You can't achieve something you don't have control over. And also, it has to mean something for you to give you the necessary motivation.

"Pay attention to where you are going because without meaning, you might get nowhere."— ***A.A. Milne***

2. Help him select strategies to achieve his goals.

Step 5: Monitor progress and provide feedback

A good plan sets the destination and the path. Progress is a constant process of action, reflection, and adjustment of one's effort based on feedback and insight.

Positive reinforcement is an influential lever for change.

As a manager, your duty is to monitor the progress of your employee and let him know when you observe behaviors you have agreed are valuable for organization. Reinforce required behaviors.

Keep watch on projects, learning opportunities, resources, and trainings that might benefit the employee. Be resourceful.

Chapter 7: Improving Communication and Team Work

Poor communication is the root of many team problems.

Poor communication leads to significant problems in the team such as quality problems, conflicts, lost opportunities, mistakes, and missed deadlines.

This is why a leader should help his team develop communication skills.

This will lead to effective teams, where everyone brings unique talents and strengths, ideas, and opportunities. Everyone contributes to the teams' goals and the work is done effectively.

People have the opportunity to create new friendships, experience a sense of group accomplishment, and have a distribution of responsibilities. Effective communication determines the success and failure of projects requiring teams, and in the end, to the business itself.

Effective communication erases the stress and negative thoughts associated with working in an unproductive team.

It is the result of gathering people under the scepter of trust and harmony that leads to a business culture of camaraderie and success.

When we talk about effective communication skills, there are some skills we should develop to increase our team work efficiency.

Learn to Listen

As a leader, you should guide your team by encouraging the culture of listening. Listening is not the same as hearing; they should learn to listen not only to the words being spoken but also how they are being spoken and the non-verbal message sent through them.

Clarification and reflection will definitely help them understand the message without any confusion and they will be appreciated for their talent for being good listeners.

Be Aware of Other People's Emotions

Try to instill the feeling of compassion and gratitude in your team. They should be aware of what's happening in someone's life and understand the changes in temperament or productivity. Make them practice empathy.

Make them consider the emotional effect of their words and teach them how to communicate within the norms of behavior acceptable to the other person.

Empathize

The ability of understanding and sharing another person's emotions and experiences should be one of the priorities of effective communication.

When communicating with others, they should not be judgmental or biased by preconceived ideas or beliefs. Instead, you should teach them how to view the situation and response from the other person's perspcctive.

Encourage

As a leader, not only should you encourage your team, but you should also cultivate the culture of understanding and encouragement between them.

Make them feel valued and appreciated through the way you communicate with them and they will definitely adopt this habit.

Effective communication is highly linked to the way we communicate our ideas, so instead of saying the first that comes into your head, you should take a moment and pay attention to what you want to say and the way you should express your ideas.

The main aspect you should focus on is what you want to communicate.

Aim to enhance the understanding by taking into account how your message might be received by the other person.

By communicating clearly, you will avoid the misreading and potential conflicts with others.

Maturity and intelligence should be the first aspects derived from your way of speaking.

You should be also very aware of the body language, the non-verbal channels of communication. You should maintain visual contact and avoid defensive body language.

The most important things you should consider in a conversation are the difference of culture, past experiences, attitudes, and abilities before transmitting your message.

Use Humor

Laughter is contagious. It can relieve stress and anxiety. Most people love to laugh and feel amazing when someone can make them laugh.

You should not be reserved in being funny or clever, but make sure the person next to you can understand your humor.

You can use the humor for breaking the ice, erasing or lowering barriers, and to get the affection of others.

Charisma should be always one of your trumps in developing relationships.

Treat People Equally

Always aim to communicate equally. Do not develop favorites and do not talk about others behind their backs. Equal treatment will bring trust and respect from others. As a leader, you will be an example to be followed.

You should also check to ensure your message was clearly understood to avoid confusion and negative thoughts.

You should encourage your team to be honest and open to feedback. Feedback is useful for building strong teams and it also can help individuals discover their deficiencies and fix them.

Attempt to Solve Conflicts

As a leader, you should troubleshoot and resolve problems the moment they arise. You should learn to be an effective mediator and negotiator. Your listening skills should help you hear and understand both parts of the argument, encouraging people start talking to each other.

Maintain a Positive Attitude and Smile

If you're asking yourself how many people will stay around a person who is miserable, the answer will be few or no one. Why? Because people need to be surrounded by positive, cheerful characters, who always stay optimistic, even in hard times, when you have to deal with challenging situations. Being positive will make others respond positively to you.

Minimize Stress

Stress is a major barrier in the communication process. It can influence your thoughts, your attitude towards the person you're talking with, and even your actions. If someone gets you angry, you should not complain in that moment, you should wait few minutes to become calm and analyze the situation with clear eyes. Try to find some positive aspects to the situation and avoid giving unnecessary criticism.

Chapter 8: Coaching Teams for Increasing Performance

Coaching is the process of improving peoples' performance, developing skills and abilities, solving problems, and helping them to face challenges and embrace changes.

Effective managers invest their time in coaching, mentoring, and developing their people.

They know that the teams are the force that drives most organizations, so they focus their energy on improving the productivity of the teams by improving relationships, concentrating on interpersonal skills and interactions, instead of on developing individuals.

No matter what type of team you are leading, what really matters is how efficient your team works. If the members of your team don't work well together, the performance and productivity can suffer.

Hostility, conflicting goals, and unclear expectations are the principal effects of an unhealthy team.

Team coaching may seem like the most effective method for improving the team performance. It will help people understand how to work better with others, reducing the conflicts and mending working relationships.

Team coaching is not only a valuable activity of making people to work together productively, but it is also an excellent and essential management and leadership tool.

Team coaching is an act of leadership in its right.

Even if team coaching has a meaningful impact on the performance of the team, recent evidence suggests that leaders focus their attention less on team coaching than on other aspects of their team leadership portfolio. They structure the team and establish its purposes, set the resources necessary for the team work, remove organizational roadblocks that can impede the work, help individual members to strengthen their personal input in the team, and work with the team as a whole to manage the use of resources and to avoid resource waste.

They allocate less attention to team coaching because they underestimate the potential benefits of providing this type of help.

The main reasons for avoiding this technique might be the lack of knowledge about coaching. Maybe leaders don't know the steps or they have already ventured a coaching intervention or two that have finished without the expected results so they started to focus on more productive ways of managing team success.

Understand the Team Dynamics

"The biggest challenge to a new employee in any company is to understand the various dynamics of how people work together."

The group dynamics are described as the results/effects of the roles and behaviors people take within the team and what the team becomes.

A team with a positive dynamic is really easy to spot: The team members trust each other, they encourage the process of receiving and giving feedback for improving skills and effectiveness, and they work toward a collective goal using a specific direction.

They hold themselves accountable for achieving the main goals. The most important aspect of a team with positive dynamics is enhanced creativity.

The members of the group are more creative because they are inspired by the team values. They can express their thoughts without reticence or fear that someone will laugh or criticize their ideas.

In a group with negative group dynamics, people can't make any decisions or accomplish any task efficiently because they can't reach a common point.

The Main Barriers of Effective Group Dynamics

Leaders can negatively contribute to the group dynamics by:

Weak leadership - When the team lacks a strong leader who can take attitude and motivate members, a person with a dominant character can easily take his place.

Lack of direction, focus on wrong objectives, and the fights between team members are the direct result of a team that is not coordinated by a capable leader.

Excessive submission to authority - When the authority of the leader undermines members' ideas and contributions, they will agree with the leader and hold back from expressing their ideas freely.

Blocking - When the team members act in a way that destroys the flow of information in the group.

There are 5 types of blocking roles:

- The joker - The person who makes jokes at inappropriate moments.
- The withdrawer - The one who doesn't contribute to group decisions or discussions.
- The aggressor - The one who disagrees most of the time with others.
- The negator - The person who always criticizes people's ideas.
- The recognition seeker - The person who seeks recognition for his ideas and who wants to be in the center of everyone's attention.

Free riding - When some members of the group leave the work for others. They may have huge contributions when they work by themselves, but in the middle of the group, they become really lazy.

Evaluation apprehension - When people think that the feedback given by the other members is too harsh and they think that instead of having a productive result, it is made to judge. They will hold back their decisions because of the fear of being judged again.

How Leaders Can Improve Team Dynamics

Once you have discovered the factors that lead to negative team dynamics, you can improve it by using the following techniques:

- **Know your team -** As a leader, your priority should be the monitoring of the team development process. You should understand the values and the behaviors that characterize the team and act in concordance with the values they stand for. Another aspect you should determine is the blocking roles and change the attitude before they start to destroy the unity of your team.

- **Tackle problems efficiently** - As a leader, you should block the destructive behaviors of team members. Give appropriate feedback that shows how this type of behavior is influencing the action he takes and show him ways to change it.

- **Define roles and responsibilities** - The lack of direction and objectives can make people to act chaotically. This leads to poor team dynamics. Everyone is trying to define or find his place in the organization and his role in the project, without any consensus. As a leader, your responsibility is to determine the roles and engage people in the process by giving them tasks to accomplish. This is called work discipline. It enhances efficiency.

- **Break down barriers** - Use feedback and team-building exercises to improve communication and help people get to know each other. At the beginning, there will be people who will reject others just because they are different. Maybe they are of another nationality, or have different habits or opinions. Your duty is to break the barriers of criticism and help people understand each other's differences and conceptions.

- **Focus on communication** - It is the key element that makes a team strong. It fosters understanding, strengthens relationships, improves teamwork, and builds trust.

- **Pay attention** - Unanimous decisions are a relevant sign of group with poor dynamics. As a leader, you should be always present in the process of making decisions within the group. If this is not possible, you should encourage the team to choose a delegator who will represent their group decisions.

This will give your team a better understanding of why they react to their colleagues in certain ways; it will foster tolerance by helping them understand that different approaches can be valid in different situations.

With a greater level of understanding, every member of your team will adjust his behavior and understand others' behavior with more comprehension and empathy.

Set Behavioral Expectations

One of the most effective ways of improving the relationships with your team and the existing relationship within the team is to understand people's perspectives.

Team coaching should provide a strict set of behaviors and communication expectations that will establish the team objectives in concordance to individual needs and preferences.

Work in the team can turn into an amazing experience if the team members work well together. If there is a lack of direction, the experience can be the worst. People will choose to set distinct directions, which leads to focusing on the wrong objectives, ineffective use of resources, and a stressful work environment.

Using the Team Charters technique, you can establish the purpose of the team, how it will work, and the desired outcomes.

The appropriate moment to create a team charter is the moment you actually create the teams.

This will provide the direction of the team during the process and the way they should behave and act to perceive the team objectives.

The Team Charter is structured into seven standpoints:

- Context - It presents the reason the team was formed, the problem that needs to be solved, how the problem is directly linked with the main objectives of the organization, and the consequences of not solving the existing issue.

- Mission and Objectives - Without a clear mission, the team will pursue only the daily objectives. The mission is defined by measurable goals and objectives. When a leader sets the goals, he has to respect the SMART framework – Specific, Measurable, Attainable, Relevant and Time-bounded. They represent the milestones of the team direction.

- Composition and Roles- As I have mentioned before, a leader has to increase team effectiveness by defining team roles and responsibilities, considering the skills and the experience of the team members and the skills required for accomplishing a certain task. Remember that employees will bring experience and approaches from different backgrounds.

- Authority and Boundaries - As a leader, the next step is to determine the time necessary for each task and prioritize the most important one. Then, you have to set the budget in terms of money and time.

- Resources and Support - Once you have set the budget, you should monitor the use of it regularly. If the team needs coaching or training, you have to provide them with permanent support.

- Operations- They are the day-to-day activities that contribute to the achievement of the final objective. You can determine just a part of the entire process or create a comprehensive and detailed list of tasks for long-term.

- Negotiation and Agreement - This technique always ends with negotiation. This means that you will negotiate the terms of the mission with your team. You have set the context and mission, objectives, composition, roles, boundaries, and resources, and now you have to ensure that the mission is achievable and your team has the necessary resources to fulfill it.

  It makes people become more committed to the process because their ideas are important to leaders and they feel respected. They realize that their ideas really count in the organization. It creates accountability.

Evaluate Reward and Recognition System

Pay has been described as the most important motivator of organizational membership and performance.

Managers were interested in increasing the employee effectiveness through financial stimulators, but it was discovered that money doesn't influence the way employees behave on a daily basis 100%.

In an organization where people work in teams and the reward system is based on individual performance, on the context of existing competing values, many employees may change their behaviors, leading to organizational problems.

Their changes in behavior are triggered by the existence of reward differences.

Money is not the only cause of dissatisfaction.

The recognition the efficient employee receives from others makes the rest of them feel undervalued.

This problem will be reflected in the performance of their work.

To avoid this problem, your reward system should be designed in a way that satisfies all employees.

Recognize everyone involved in the pursuit of the goal, while looking for a reason you believe that person had a positive and significant influence in the process. Reward them the moment they come up with a brilliant input.

This behavior makes people increase their performance.

Verbal recognition in front of the team signifies more than the material incentive they receive through the performance system.

Another factor that influences employee behavior is the discrepancy between the organization's goals and individual goals. When you notice this type of problem, an individual session of coaching is the perfect way to manage the situation, to align the employee's goals with the team mission.

Determine what motivates him to work effectively for company's goals. Find out if he has personal difficulties that may interfere in the work process and influence his performance.

Support Individual Development

One of the main responsibilities of a manager/leader is to help his team with the professional and career development.

As a manager, you should provide opportunities for them to develop the knowledge, skills, abilities, tools, and resources to become a professional in their job and career.

The most useful techniques you can use in the process of developing your team members are:

- Provide on-the-job training and coaching
- Give performance goals and feedback
- Support the development goals
- Help them write an individual development plan

The last point doesn't refer on redacting it for your employees.

He should initiate the process and do most of the writing of the development plan.

As a leader, your duty is to meet with the employees and discuss their plans, give feedback on their ideas, provide suggestions for their development activities, help them set realistic goals/objectives and determine potential obstacles, schedule regular meetings to monitor progress, make revisions of the plan, and see the final results.

The individual development plan should look like this:

Individual Development Plan

Name: Position:

Department: Supervisor:

Date:

Goals To be achieved (from performance plan)	Skills or Competencies To be learned or acquired	Resources What is needed (money, time, etc.)	Activities Possible learning opportunities to try	Status (Start/Completed Results)
Short-range Critical within present position (1 Year)				
Mid-range Important for growth within present position (2 Years)				
Long-range Helpful for achieving career goals (3-5 Years)				

Chapter 9: The Model of Effective Management

Effective management is based on achieving performance and results, taking advantage of the full engagement of a committed and motivated team.

The effectiveness of the management process is influenced by significant factors, such as the external environment, like personality, culture, and experience, and internal factors like the vision, history, dimensions of the company, the stability of values, and thinking.

Effective managers hold themselves and others accountable. It means that they account for, and explain, their actions and the use of human and financial resources entrusted to them.

They operate on the basis of values, including them in the day-to-day activities and decisions. They are aware of the importance of following these values because they have to be a positive example for employees.

Effective managers are motivated and enabled by their emotional, conceptual, and technical competences, managing actions, changes, and people, exceeding the organizational boundaries for achieving highly substantial results.

They have an acute sense of their personal values, using them as an inner compass that ensures the alignment of their actions with their values. Their image stands in the ability of being transparent and always being an example for their teams.

Emotional competence is the most important factor that contributes to effectiveness. It implies managing oneself and the relationship with others. The most difficult aspect is dealing with people and creating strong bonds with them. They need to be patient and open to embracing new mentalities, cultures, and behaviors; they need to understand people who come from different environments because their habits are mostly based on the experience they have had before.

They are self-aware, managing their emotions and the influence they have on others. They create a positive, dynamic work environment, involving teams in the process of making decisions, listening to their opinions and problems, solving the existing conflicts, or anticipating future ruptures and fixing them before they turn into real problems. This kind of attitude brings the team recognition and contribution to the work goals.

Conceptual competence is fundamental for managers to create the perspective of what is happening around them (where they are in the present) and to establish the level they want to reach in future (where they want to go).

Conceptual competence allows them to determine patterns of actions, emerging trends and how to approach them, and the context for change and how it can be successfully implemented in the organization.

Technical competence guarantees the implementation of technical knowledge in the process of achieving objectives in ways that benefit their work group and the organization as a whole. It implies sharing their knowledge and building knowledge networks, as well as developing themselves and others.

There are three core values for managers.

These core values have different phases of performance, depending on the level of responsibility a manager has: Middle managers, senior manager, and organizational leader.

Integrity is determined by the level morality a manager has, how strong his moral principles are.

The integrity for middle managers is characterized by applying the core values in making decisions and clarifying choices.

It means to act as a role model for your team, showing them every day how your actions reflect your principles and ethical behavior.

They are concerned about respecting the ethics, even in a hard situation, when people can't respect them or they are too stressed to consider them. An organizational leader will guide them every time and he will make sure that the ethics are respected.

The integrity doesn't mean only being ethical at work and in your relationships, it also means to respect your word and your responsibilities, to be counted on to do what you say. Because words are easy, like the wind...they are just a proof of what you want to be, but your actions prove who you really are.

People will always watch for actions, not for your intentions. Your actions and your words should always agree with each other.

Any discordance between them makes people believe that you are pretending and you are not a good example to follow or a good leader to be respected and trusted. Your integrity is mirrored when your actions fit your given word perfectly.

Senior managers protect fairness and identify and avoid conflicts of interest, maintaining the neutrality between teams.

They chase their goals and they are very resilient to external pressures and conflicts.

Integrity is reflected in their moral attitudes, when they do the right thing for the right reasons and they try to persuade others to do so as well.

They are really open to sharing information and knowledge with their teams and they involve their crew in the process of making decisions, considering each idea and rewarding people for being active in the process. They take credit for someone's contribution.

Integrity for organizational leaders is mirrored in their intention to build departmental and organizational cultures that follow the moral beliefs and ethics.

They have no tolerance for the treading of integrity in the personal and systemic levels.

Integrity has a different meaning for each type of manager, because they have different responsibilities and they are acting in distinct levels of power, but they maintain the main idea of integrity and check if the moral values are respected and take action to increase team awareness towards morality and ethics.

Professionalism is defined as the conducts, aims, or qualities that characterize or mark a profession or a professional person. It is based on specialized knowledge, intensive academic preparation, competency, honesty, and integrity.

For middle managers, professionalism is based on respecting the basic professional discipline: punctuality, the schedule, and appropriate use of office equipment and telephones. They are focused on defining the performance expectations for their teams and the quality standards of their work.

Mostly focused on achieving results, they are really conscious, decisive, and efficient at work, being able to make firm decisions in times of pressure or uncertainty.

Senior managers see professionalism as a way of respecting schedules for meetings and deadlines, achieving big results.

They are always seeking the improvement of the work quality, creating a positive, stimulating environment for employees.

Their meaningful concern is the rational use of resources.

Organizational leaders understand professionalism as a way of enforcing organizational standards of professional behavior.

The culture of excellence is their ultimate purpose.

Respect for diversity means to understand that each individual has something called uniqueness and to recognize the individual differences.

Diversity has so many dimensions: Race, ethnicity, gender, sexual orientation, socio-economic status, age, physical abilities, religious beliefs, political beliefs, or other ideologies.

Middle managers are very sensitive to group differences and they understand the lack of homogeneity between people's views and ideas.

They communicate their views without forcing people to consider them as the only solution to problems.

They see diversity as an opportunity to learn new things and hear new perspectives from different cultures and mentalities.

They know that "strength lies in differences, not in similarities."— Stephan R. Covey.

Senior managers build a diversified work force.

They ensure that the diversity is respected, acting to diminish biases and intolerance.

Organizational managers take advantage of diversity for achieving outstanding results, increasing creativity, and defining innovations.

Chapter 10: The Main Pillars of Emotional Competence

Effective management is based on the performance of managers, on their ability to focus their attention and effort in a well-balanced way on different domains. They manage people, they manage actions and changes, protruding the organization barriers, building relationships with stakeholders, partners, directors, and subordinates, leveraging the external and internal networks.

There are eight pillars of emotional competence, which indicate the awareness of managers regarding their values and the way they act, creating a climate of openness and confidence.

1. **Self-awareness** means to have a concrete perspective of your personality, including strengths, weaknesses, thoughts, beliefs, behaviors, emotions, and motivation. It makes you understand people's feelings and actions, it keeps you away from judging people, and it helps you make changes in the thoughts and interpretations you make in your mind. Changing interpretations helps you change your emotions and control your mind and attitudes toward people or actions.

When you master it, you're capable of influencing your entire life, because it is your attention, emotions, reactions, personality, and thoughts that determine where you go in life.

People with weak self-awareness don't have a clear understanding of their potential; this is why they mostly fail in accomplishing their dreams.

Self-awareness determines your ability to communicate and create strong relationships in your personal life as well as in the workplace. Empathy is one of the results of self-awareness. It helps you understand people's reactions and the reason behind them.

Managers are aware of how their emotions affect their performance. They try to create a positive and productive climate for their teams, even in times of pressure or uncertainty.

Even if they are stressed because of the workloads or deadlines, they need to support their teams and show them a debonair attitude, motivating people to work efficiently.

Self-awareness helps managers determine their strengths and uncover their weaknesses.

2. Self-confidence is a feeling or consciousness of the powers or of the reliance on circumstances, faith, or belief that you will act in a right, proper, or effective way. It is the belief that you have the ability and knowledge to succeed.

Confidence is a tremendous tool for influencing people. Your confidence can inspire confidence in others (bosses, clients, audiences, peers, and most importantly, your team).

Gaining the confidence of the team is one of the key ways a self-confident person finds success.

Self-assurance is a desideratum of self-confidence and managers are aware of its presence.

Managers are very decisive and confident in their abilities to make firm decisions in every context.

3. Emotional self-control is the ability to control your emotions, behavior, and desires in the face of external demands, to function in society.

Self-control is about making our failures pale in contrast to our successes. But it is difficult to do so when we don't know we possess this strength within us. Self-control is a skill we all possess, yet we tend to give ourselves little credit for it.

The central point of failure in achieving success in life is self-control. Our modern society suffers from the lack of self-control. Most of the problems that exist in our society, such as addiction, overeating, crime, domestic violence, sexually transmitted diseases, prejudice, debt, unwanted pregnancy, educational failure, underperformance at school and work, lack of savings, and failure to exercise have the absence or the deficiency of self-control in common because control is the ability of suppressing impulses and faulty actions.

Self-control helps managers to stay calm and positive even in difficult situations. It helps them handle difficult people and tense situations with diplomacy and tact, avoiding stress and uncertainty.

It supports them in being consistent in their behavior with others in their personal and business life.

4. Conscientiousness is a fundamental personality trait that influences people to make and keep the long-term goals or respect obligations and reflect over the choices they have to make in life.

Conscientiousness is a key element for success...Why? Because conscientious people are very organized and responsible, working hard to face challenges and control impulses that can destroy their image or shadow their personality.

They are really good at setting goals because they set that goal, work toward it, and persist amid setbacks. If they can't accomplish it, they set more attainable goals, trying to achieve them rather than becoming discouraged or giving up. They succeed despite hindrances.

Conscientious people always have a backup plan. Even if they fail, they have a plan to deal with failure.

For conscientious people, persistency heavily influences their success.

This is why conscientious managers respect promises and meet commitments. They are very organized and careful in their work, checking twice for mistakes. The most important aspect is they admit their mistakes instead of reacting defensively.

5. Optimism is the feeling of hopefulness and confidence someone feels about the future or the success of an action.

Optimists have a clear or innate tendency to make lemonade out of lemons, whereas pessimists complain about it. They see the glass as half-full rather than half-empty.

The quality of a person's life is mostly influenced by the way they perceive it, its ups and downs, the way they interpret the changes that happen in their lives, and the attitude they take toward it.

An optimistic outlook is healthy for your body and your relationships.

It doesn't mean ignoring the hard or challenging parts of life, it means to change the way you approach them. Mindfulness and patience are ingredients of optimism and they make you find new perspectives and paths.

Optimistic managers focus more on solutions than on problems. They see possibilities and opportunities rather than obstacles.

When they have to face a problem, they adopt an energetic and enthusiastic attitude rather than being discouraged and complaining about the difficulty of a hindrance.

They focus more on creating a favorable climate for their teams, encouraging them to perceive problems as ways to develop their aptitudes and skills.

6. Achievement orientation is a drive to accomplish goals and meet or exceed a high standard of success.

It is the quality of striving hard to achieve something.

Achievement-oriented people tend to be leaders because they are tactical and strategic thinkers, they are always looking for situations when people gravitate toward them.

Their main objective is the high-quality work, which is why they make sure everyone respects the tasks they were charged with and verify the performance of it.

They take responsibility for their actions, decisions, and mistakes. If they make mistakes, they blame no one but themselves.

They are very resilient, which means that they will never give up. They will try to find another strategy or approach until they succeed.

Achievement-oriented people set high standards. They are continually seeking ways to improve their skills and performance. They understand the necessity of cultivating constant learning and improvement.

Commitment is the key ingredient that defines the character of an achievement-oriented manager.

7. Empathy is the awareness of the feelings and emotions of others.

It is the power of protruding someone else's personality and imaginatively feeling his experiences.

It is the binder between self and others.

Managers with a high level of empathy show sensitivity and understand others' perspectives. They pay considerable attention to non-verbal communication.

They are good listeners, being able to help others based on their understanding of people's needs and feelings.

8. Discretion means to respect the privacy of others and keep confidential things confidential.

It means to respect the boundaries between the personal and professional issues and misunderstandings between people.

Chapter 11: The Main Pillars of Conceptual Competence

Companies face demographic shifts, new rivals, new technologies, new regulations, or other environmental changes that seems to come out of nowhere and become decisive aspects.

Conceptual competence is the ability to identify patterns and connections between situations that are not visibly related, identifying ways to solve issues in complex situations.

The means for a company to be successful in a globally competitive market lies in the power of managers to visualize what may not be apparent, then delegate the task of strategy implementation to the other levels of management.

Effective managers have peripheral vision, which means that they have the ability to understand or visualize the weak signals at the periphery, the blurry zone at the edge of an organization's vision.

The success or survival of a company is directly linked to understanding or interpreting these signals.

Managers are used to analyze data set before them, but they also need to know what piece of the big puzzle is missing.

They need to ask themselves, ***"What don't we know that might matter?"***

Maybe the past is not a reliable predictor of the future, but it might unveil blind spots of the company that will affect its performance in the near future.

Effective managers analyze social, technological, economic, political, and environmental changes that occurred in the past to try to determine the major consequences they have had for the company and how it has responded to these external changes, identifying persistent blind spots that might cause another collapse in the future.

They have to determine and eliminate the root causes of the blind spots.

Benchmarking against the past is a starting point, a way to catch up and reduce the vulnerability to surprises.

But to truly benefit from the periphery in a competitive sense, managers will also need to examine the present and future.

It has been proved that we filter and ignore a huge amount of information that might be decisive for increasing performance. We might exclude essential information from our perception. This is one of our most powerful tendencies, but managers should be aware of this. They should seek insight into these signals in the organization and determine the level of attention each signal needs.

The mission of this analysis is to determine outside factors that can threaten the core of the organization.

Important signals can be identified by selecting a signal and fast-advancing its development using scenario planning or future-mapping techniques.

Another strategy is to consider what mavericks and outliers are trying to tell you about the business you're managing.

They are either people from your organization, employees with a strong ability to determine ruptures and shifts, with insights about the periphery of the organization. Outliers with a huge amount of knowledge about new customers and technologies that might replace the current ones can give you an idea of the blind spots you're missing.

Effective leaders organize meetings with their employees to get their views and opinions and gather news and information about the environment. This way, they discover the weak signals from the periphery of their vision.

There are three main pillars effective managers use to consolidate their management:

Use of concepts

Effective managers explain important events that occur in the organization using concepts, frameworks, or theory.

They have an adaptive capacity, developing new concepts and frameworks to explain their vision and reflect the linkages between ideas and concepts.

They find similarities between actual situations and past situations, designing new frameworks to explain these similarities.

Effective managers determine the discrepancies and variations between the desired and the real result of a situation.

Systems thinking

It is a holistic approach that concentrates on the way parts of a system interrelate and how the system works over time in the condition of being integrated in another larger system.

Although almost 95% of the people are event oriented, which means that each event has a cause and if they want to solve the problem, they have to find the cause of it and fix it, effective managers see the problem entirely different. They perceive the structure of the system as being the determinant of the problem.

There are fourteen steps of systems thinking:

1. **The big picture** - A system thinker analyzes the dynamics of a system and the relationships among its parts. They catch the whole picture, not its components.

2. **Change over time** - The dynamic system is created from independent elements, the values of which change over time. The changes are generating trends and patterns that are analyzed by the system thinker.

3. **System's structure -** A system thinker knows that the system's structure determines its behavior.

4. **Interdependencies** - The cause-effect relationships within the dynamic system have a circular nature. It is based on feedback, trying to reach and maintain a specific goal.

5. **Connections** - Each new connection has a meaningful impact in supporting a better understanding of the relationships in the system. The process of learning is made by integrating new knowledge with current understanding. The new information connects to the previous knowledge by adding, modifying, transferring, and synthesizing the information into a deeper understanding.

6. **Change perspectives** - The process of understanding a dynamic system has to be made from a variety of different angles and points of view.

7. **Assumptions** - They help a systems thinker to understand how the system works. This leads to improved performance.

8. **Considers issues fully** - The system thinker is focused on understanding the structure and the behavior of the system. They don't urge to take hurried solutions to problems because they can't be completely analyzed and their underperformance can influence the system long-term.

9. **Mental models** - Every situation provides the opportunity for an individual to perceive or interpret what is happening, creating the big picture of the event. The mental models are ideas, assumptions, or values that sometimes resist for a lifetime. This is why systems thinkers

are aware of the importance of mental models and try to be very objective in creating them because they can affect the actions they ultimately make.

10. Leverage - Based on the knowledge a systems thinker has about the structure, interdependencies, and vision of the system, he can implement the leverage action that will lead to desirable results.

11. Consequences - Before taking any action, a systems thinker will analyze the potential consequences of his actions and the probability of the chosen action to produce the desired outcome.

12. Accumulations - They are a component of the system and they have rates of change that can vary over time.

13. **Time delays** - When an action is taken in a dynamic system, the outcome will appear after a while. Time delays have a significant impact on the performance of the system.

14. **Successive approximation** - It is a series of rewards that provide positive reinforcement for behavior changes that are successive steps towards the final desired behavior. In systems thinking, successive approximation refers to the ability of checking results and changing actions when needed.

Systems thinkers have the courage of making adjustments, try new approaches when they are striving for high performance (long-term goals), and even sacrifice the short-term goals, risking poor results.

The more they learn, the more they discover how much is truly unknown or misunderstood.

The quest for understanding more becomes a continuing process of successive approximation.

The process requires patience, which is challenging because of the pressures of achieving immediate, visible, desired results.

Long-term, noticeable improvements take time and they won't be accomplished by making quick decisions or taking fast actions. They occur as a result of sage decisions and strategic implementation.

Pattern recognition

The third pillar of conceptual competence is related to the identification of patterns in the amount of unorganized information or random data.

Effective managers have the ability to unravel the big picture of the company from chaotic information and shape the strategy that will guide them along the way.

They use concepts and similarities to understand or explain different situations or new patterns.

Chapter 12: The Main Pillars of Technical Competence

Technical competence is the ability to perform in activities after a defined standard. It is based on knowledge, expertise, and skills that help a manager to successfully accomplish a task.

An effective manager can achieve the desired result only guided by the following concepts:

Knowledge and information management is the process of capturing, distributing, and effectively using knowledge.

It helps managers share information and knowledge within the organization.

Knowledge management is about connecting people to people, information, and tools through technology and process.

Knowledge management facilitates the right distribution of information to the right person at the right time.

Middle managers are aware of how knowledge and information can influence their roles in the organization.

They use expertise to control the whole organization and solve problems, using a unique problem-solving strategy that involves knowledge and technology.

Senior managers share their knowledge and information through management strategies, ensuring that their strategies are involved in the key processes of the company.

Organizational leaders develop a culture based on the knowledge and information they have gained. The vision of the company relies on knowledge.

Knowledge network is the effective way of integrating individuals' knowledge and skill in the pursuit of personal and organizational objectives.

The concept compounds the idea of sharing, developing, and evolving under the authority of knowledge.

Knowledge networks focus their attention on people and information as the most valuable resources a company has in the era of tough global competition.

Organizations are looking for ways to generate extra value from their assets and knowledge can make the difference in making a competitive advantage. This is why knowledge management plays a crucial role in leveraging the efficiency.

Knowledge networks encourage better communication and collaboration between teams, making the assimilation of the new knowledge, information, insights, and ideas an easy process for organizations.

They create, transfer, absorb, share, and leverage information at higher rates because their culture encourages them to nurture communication and a highly effective transfer of knowledge, leading to efficient implementation of new strategies that create a competitive advantage.

Knowledge sharing

It is said that one of the most challenging aspects of knowledge management is to convince people to share their knowledge with their group.

How can you get people to share their hard-won knowledge when they consider it a personal advantage?

Why don't people share?

Because "knowledge is power" and people are really conscious of its significance.

Because they don't trust other people. They believe that sharing their knowledge with others will make them vulnerable or others will take their concepts and implement them as if it were their own.

Because people don't have time to share. There is pressure on productivity or deadlines that encourages highly skilled people to learn more, to become more productive but at the same time, it isolates them from the rest of the group because knowledge requires time to be assimilated. This leaves less time for sharing sessions with their teams.

Because they don't realize how beneficial sharing is. To make people realize how beneficial is for them, you have to encourage them to share.

There are three ways to encourage people to share their knowledge:

Make it safe

This means to create the perfect environment for knowledge sharing, where people are reassured that they won't be at risk if they make their ideas and abilities visible to others. The denial of sharing comes from job insecurities or from the fear of becoming vulnerable. The more people know about you, the more powerless you become.

As a manager, you have to assure them that sharing knowledge will make them powerful and confident in the forces they hold within.

Make it count

This means to motivate people to share by introducing a reward system. A relevant example is making it a key factor in the annual performance review of individuals.

Make it social

This means to leverage the standards of sharing knowledge, making it a social experience. People adore sharing things with others when they are in the middle of a group and they can capture the attention because it makes them feel motivated, respected, self-satisfied, confident, and admired. They feel that their work counts and their ideas are appreciated by others. The social context also provides an intrinsic reward that can be even more motivating than the performance rewards.

Continuous Learning and Development

"Learning and innovation go hand in hand. The arrogance of success is to think that what you did yesterday will be sufficient for tomorrow."

The process of learning has the same end as life does: Death. It is your choice if you want to live it until the end, but it can make a difference in your life.

Continuous learning is about the constant expansion of skills, development of abilities and competences, and increase of knowledge.

Effective managers are the militants of learning because they develop their learning approach in their day-to-day work.

They seek opportunities to develop new skills and learn new strategies.

They promote the systems, processes, and mechanisms that contribute to continuous learning and development because they are interested in infusing this lifestyle into their people.

They provide the necessary resources to make the process more fruitful/effective.

Chapter 13: Emotional Intelligence: The Binder between Leadership and Management

Maybe you have noticed people who are really good listeners, who, no matter what kind of situation they are in, they know how to act and what to say, so that people won't get offended or upset about it.

We may have also noticed people who are really skilled at hiding their real emotions. They master and manage them with tact, optimism, and realism.

They don't become anxious or stressed. Instead, they have the ability to assess the problem calmly and find the best solutions to every problem. They are very good decision makers and they know when to follow their intuition.

They even encourage criticism as an opportunity to improve their performance.

What separates them from common people? What makes them so unique in term of character, behavior, and personality?

They have a high degree of emotional intelligence. They know themselves very well and they are capable of understanding people's emotions.

Emotional intelligence is the ability to identify, use, understand, and manage emotions in positive ways to relieve stress, communicate effectively, empathize with others, overcome challenges, and defuse conflict, as scientists say.

Emotional intelligence becomes a fundamental factor in defining the success in life.

People with a high level of emotional intelligence are more likely to succeed because they have strong tools that make them stand out.

They react with kindness and sympathy; they help others when they have the opportunity to do so.

This is why they get help easily when they ask for it, and this is why others want them as team members or team leaders.

Characteristics of Emotional Intelligence

There is a suggestive framework of the elements that constitutes emotional intelligence:

1. ***Self-awareness*** - People with a high level of EI are very self-aware. Their life stands under the rules of objectivity because they don't let their emotions influence their lucidity. Very confident people, they trust their intuition and act out of the control of their emotions. They also have a very developed cult of personality, mastering their strengths, and acknowledging their weaknesses. They are constantly improving their performance.

2. **Self-regulation** - It is the ability of controlling impulses and emotions. Most people with this ability don't become angry as fast, they even block this feeling. They are very calculated, being very careful when they make important decisions. They don't act impulsively. The fundamental characteristics of self-regulated people

are integrity, the ability to say no, thoughtfulness, and the ability to embrace change.

3. **Motivation** - People with EI are very motivated to achieve long-term success. They not only want this, but they also take action to accomplish their goals. One of the main characteristics is the passion for challenges.

4. **Empathy** - After self-awareness, this is the most important element of EI. It is the ability to identify with, and understand, people's needs, feelings, viewpoints, and desires. People with an increased level of empathy are very skilled at recognizing others' feelings even if they are not so obvious. This is why they are very good at managing people and listening.

5. **Social skills -** Maybe you have noticed people who are really easy to talk to because they don't judge, they understand, and they try to help you as much as they can. They are excellent communicators, focusing more on helping others than on their success. For them, success comes as a side effect.

Emotional Intelligence is a key element that contributes to success in life, especially in people's careers. Developing and using EI is a sign that you can become a great leader.

How to Develop Your Emotional Intelligence

For some people, emotional intelligence is an innate ability, but for the majority, it is an ability that can be learned and developed.

The following techniques will help you work on 5 areas of emotional intelligence:

- ***Analyze your reaction and the way you communicate with others.*** Are you the kind of person who rushes to judge before hearing all the facts? Do you stereotype? Try to be very honest when you think about it. Try to put yourself in their place. Maybe you will understand that you have to be more open and accept others' opinions and perspectives.

- ***Examine your work environment.*** Do you seek attention and compliments? Humility should be one of your qualities. It doesn't mean that you are weak or self-confident when you receive attention for your accomplishments, it means that you are confident enough to realize what you did. You should also give others the opportunity to shine, without the fear of not receiving praise for yourself.

- ***Evaluate yourself.*** Determine what your strengths and weaknesses are. Will you accept that you are not perfect and there are areas you need to improve? Looking honestly at yourself is the first step in changing your behavior and as a result, your life.

- ***Examine your response and behavior in stressful situations.*** Do you get upset every time there is a delay or things don't happen as you wish? Do you blame others for your failures? One of the most appreciated abilities in business today is resisting under stressful conditions. Try to master your emotions when things go wrong.

- ***Take responsibility for your actions.*** If you have made a mistake or hurt someone's feelings, the solution to apologize. If you are honest, people will forgive you and also forget what you did.

- ***Think about how your actions will influence others.*** Try to put yourself in their place again and determine how it will impact others. What are the effects and how can you help them deal with these effects?

Remember that Emotional Intelligence is the most used technique for recruiting new employees. It has gained a huge importance over time because of its impact on people's personality and behavior in the workplace and personal situations.

Emotional Intelligence- Molder of the Leadership Process

When you think of a "perfect leader", what enters your mind?

When I think of a perfect leader, I think of a person whose actions inspire others to dream more, learn more, do more, and become more.

A perfect leader is the person who unlocks people's potential, who set high standard firstly for him and then for his team, who gives a shape to the vision, whose performance is not measured by attributes but by results, It is a person who assumes his responsibilities, who always makes careful, informed decisions, who never lets his temper get out of control, who easily gains the trust and respect of others, who listens to the team, and who is easy to talk to.

What makes the difference between a leader and a manager? Leaders nurture and enhance, whereas managers only arrange and order.

Leaders are managers with exacerbated values and beliefs, who not only tell others what to do, but also help them do it.

Leaders are managers with a high degree of emotional intelligence.

For leaders, emotional intelligence is a vital key for success.

An effective leader is the person who masters the five elements of emotional intelligence: self-awareness, self-regulation, motivation, empathy, and social skills.

The more that a leader manages each of these areas, the higher the level of emotional intelligence.

Self-awareness in Leadership

Self-aware leaders know how they feel and how their emotions and actions can affect the people around them.

Being a self-aware leader means to acknowledge your strengths and determine your opportunities and transform obstacles in new way of improving your state.

Another aspect is to act with humility in every situation, and give others the opportunity to show their abilities though performance and let them shine, without being restrained by the fear of not being praised for your brilliant performance.

How can you improve your self-awareness as a leader?

1. As a leader, an efficient way to improve your self-awareness is to **keep a journal**. Keeping a journal helps you keep track of your thoughts. You can write reactions you have had over the day at work, how you have felt in a certain situation when you were supposed to control your emotions, and your strengths and weaknesses. Your level of self-awareness will increase a lot.

2. Another method of enhancing your self-awareness is to **slow down**. What does it mean? It means that you have to slow down when you experience anger or other strong emotions that can darken your consciousness. Try to determine the reason why you're experiencing these types of negative thoughts. And keep in mind that the way you react in a particular situation is your choice. If you don't like how you behave, change your behavior. It all lies in your will.

Willpower is more influential than any negative thought that may obfuscate your mind. Self-awareness is the key factor in a leader's success because it keeps them grounded, being able to be efficient and deliberate on the task, attuned to those around them, and focused on developing employees and communicate their vision efficiently. They should be able to practice self-awareness, controlling their mind and emotions, and encouraging others to develop their knowledge and success.

3. **Keep an open mind**
   When you can control your own emotions, you can be more social with

others. Attractiveness becomes a trump card in your hands when you're more open to others.

4. **Stay focused**
Making connections with others is very important for a leader's position, but sometimes it becomes difficult because our attention is absorbed by so many distractions. As a leader, you need to train yourself to focus for long periods of time.

5. **Set boundaries**
For a leader, setting boundaries is essential to the integrity of his goals and the work he dedicates to achieve them. It is important to say "yes" when someone is asking you for help. In the end, this is your responsibility, this is why they chose you to represent and support them. But it is also to know when to say "no" with a warm attitude.

Your passions and work have to be a priority, but you can also reject people without reason or when they have to deal with a hazardous situation that needs a strategic, well thought out solution.

6. Acknowledge your emotional triggers

There is a myriad of challenges you can encounter in your life and each challenge is followed by a particular feeling: frustration, anger, sadness, and embarrassment. Some of these feelings can be draining or frustrating and they can influence the way we respond to our challenges.

They can lead to actions that we will regret after taking them such as debates, strong arguments, expressing things that we later wish we hadn't, freezing up in fear, or leaving without trying. Some of these triggers have a rooted background in our early lives. Some of them might be the results of what happened in the past when you were a kid.

Some of them originate from our core beliefs and values. You may become really angry when you see people cheating or some of your colleagues are making fun of another colleague because he is of another nationality or religion or beliefs. If your values reject the racism, you will definitely become angry when you are a witness of the moral violation. As a leader, you will encounter a huge amount of triggers, such as people coming late to the meeting you have scheduled, lack of openness to alternative possibilities, the lack of accountability, or untruthful people.

These are the main buttons that evoke negative emotions. By knowing our emotional triggers, we can explore, manage, and increase the potential of emotional resilience. By identifying your triggers, you become more empowered. It enhances your self-awareness, which leads to different actions. Your actions become more aligned to your values and visions. Self-aware leaders are able to identify their emotions when they are happening. Self-awareness linked to your triggers is not about repressing the reactions and their causes, it is about being able to bend and flex with them, and fully process them before communicating with others. The more aware you are of your triggers, the less control they have over you.

7. Embrace your intuition

"Have the courage to follow your heart and intuition. They somehow already know what you truly want to become. Everything else is secondary." - **Steve Jobs**

Leaders are people who trust their own inner guidance more than others.

In the middle of confusion, when they have to make decisive choices, they follow their intuition, because it is more powerful than the fear of trying. It is more powerful than the fear of failing.

Intuition is not only a gut instinct, as some of us may believe, it is a conscious act of showing and unveiling what we have actually learned and we have just remembered. It is an involuntary act of bringing the knowledge we have gained over the time to the surface in a unique formula...in a unique expression, a voice without words.

Intuitive individuals are not common people, because intuition never comes to unprepared minds; it is even more powerful than intellect. It never shows up where it cannot be sustained by a creative and conscious mind.

Intuition is directly linked to success. Why?

Because intuition is connected to discovery and discovery is related to action. So, successful people trusted in their intuition in the beginning and took the risks associated with it. They made discovery after discovery. They have tried until they succeeded.

Instincts, in a different way, tell us what to do. By learning to trust and use them, you will become an inspiring leader.

8. Practice self-discipline

Strong leadership is empowered by disciplined people, not only at work, but also in their personal life.

Self-discipline enables a leader to be more focused on their tasks and ideas.

Self-regulation- A Star Leader's Secret Weapon

Our emotions are moved by biological impulses.

The biological impulses are beyond our control, but our emotions are not.

Emotions can be managed by self-regulation, which saves us from being hostages to our impulses.

People with self-regulation are more inclined toward reflection and thoughtfulness, acceptance of uncertainty and change, and integrity.

People with a strong ability to control their emotions might seem cold or dispassionate, but they are more emotional intelligent than others and they can understand how their reactions can affect others.

Why is self-regulation so important in the leadership process?

1. **Fair-minded people** are people with an agile ability to control their emotions.

They are really involved in the leadership and organizational processes, so they can easily create and sustain a safe and fair environment.

They increase the productivity of the organization and reduce the possibility of future conflicts between people.

2. Self-regulation is a competitive asset

The business environment is changing rapidly as a result of the improvements in technology and company divisions and mergers every day. Managers, especially leaders, have to face these shifts in the workplace and adapt their abilities and knowledge to new business rules, new trends and mentalities, new organizational strategies, new databases, while focusing on implementation and leading the way by example.

Leaders who practice self-regulation rarely make hasty or emotional decisions, judge or stereotype others, compromise their values, or attack their people verbally. They are very skilled at managing emotions and understanding how they not only influence, but also affect others.

3. Self-regulation magnifies integrity

Integrity is a key virtue and asset in the organizational system.

There are people in the organization who want to take advantage of their position to increase their personal gain. Integrity is the key to avoid these problems within organizations.

4. Self-Motivation in Leadership

One thing you should probably know is that you can't motivate others if you can't find the power within to motivate yourself first.

Motivation is an intrinsic fire, which, at some point, goes out for burning with delightful flames.

You need to find that flame within and bring it to the surface, so people can see it and be inspired by it.

Motivation in leadership is about uplifting and inspiring people to perform at their best because they believe in your values and your ability to take a vision and transform it in reality.

But before you can inspire others, you have to inspire yourself.

The starting point is to begin seeing yourself as a role model, a person who leads people by example.

If you don't believe you are a good leader, how can others start seeing you like this if you don't inspire them to believe it?

It is the same principle as for success. What is the key to being successful? Act as if you already are.

What is the key to becoming a motivational leader? Act as if you already are one.

And this has to start from your heart.

Motivate yourself by striving toward excellence, by committing yourself to achieve everything in your power to achieve.

Start seeing yourself as the person who sets high standards that other people will follow.

Prove to them that you are right, that your standards and rules drive the organization to high achievements.

Instead of trying to make others follow your visions and beliefs, try to live a lifestyle that motivates them to follow you because they have seen amazing results from your ideas and want to become like you without you saying a word.

Who motivates the motivator?

A leader is motivated by himself.

He finds that inner strength to be excited by his ambitions and dreams every day, by his powerful visions that he turns into reality with each step he takes toward them.

How?

1. He constantly finds reasons he is doing his job.

It is very important for your self-motivation to find reasons why you have chosen that way.

In the day-to-day chaos, you might forget what you really love about your career because you have to face continual challenges and find effective answers to problems.

You not only have to solve your problems, but you also have to help others find solutions to their problems because you are leading a team.

People chose you to do this because you demonstrated that you care about their career development and you are always stretching for ways to improve their performance in different ways. People chose you because you guide them toward accomplishing the organization's goals and objectives.

They rely on you when a conflict starts or a problem arises.

You may sometimes feel exhausted and demotivated, you might forget what really represents you.

Take a moment and think about what motivated you to choose this career.

How did you find yourself in this path?

What inspires you when you think about your career?

What can you improve so that you can become more motivated?

2. Know where you stand

Determine if you are motivated enough to lead.

3. Find something good in what you are doing

Leaders are very optimistic, no matter what problems they encounter in life. Why? Because they think about the opportunity that is hiding behind the problem.

They don't perceive the problem as a negative fact that is going to influence the performance, but as an opportunity to develop new skills, try alternatives, and discover new results and new paths that go in the same direction as the initial one.

Every time you face a challenge, or even a failure, try to find at least one good aspect. The idea is to discover that in every bad situation, there is a good aspect that follows it.

Empathy: The Force That Moves Business Forward

Behind every successful organization is a leader who has mastered the skills of empathy.

Leaders establish personal and professional connections and relate to others because they need people to turn their vision into reality. They need support, they need people to work for their vision not because they are paid to do it, but because they have understood the benefits the vision brings to the organization and as a result, to the people who are working for it.

Leaders need people to be fully engaged in achieving performance and to trust their ideas. They need people to come up with input and brilliant innovations.

And what's that force that makes leaders create strong bonds with their teams? Empathy.

In its purest form, empathy drives the communication process in business. It makes people understand different opinions without repressive actions.

You know that feeling when you put yourself in someone else's shoes? You try to understand why that person acted in an inappropriate way or why he/she made that decision. In that moment, you are empathetic. You try to determine the intrinsic reasons of those actions, without judging.

This is a leader's job. They never judge people, they try to find the right reason.

How to Enhance Empathy in Leaders

1. *Put yourself in someone else's position*
2. *Pay attention to body language* because it might communicate a strong message, one that is not always a positive one. If you master body language, you will be better able to determine how others feel about a situation and learn how to respond to the problem in an appropriate way.

3. *Respond to feelings.* You might ask an employee to work overtime and even he accepts it, you can hear the disappointment in his voice. In that moment, you should try to solve it by encouraging him and appreciating his effort. Another thing you should do is to give him another free day after his

big effort. It will make him feel totally appreciated and motivated to work. When you treat people with accountability, they treat you the same way.

Social Skills in Leadership

Leaders with highly developed social skills in the area of emotional intelligence are really good communicators.

They are not only prepared to receive good news, but they also can receive bad news with the same openness.

They are really good motivators, encouraging people to work for their projects and dedicated to achieving the best results possible.

They are really good at coaching people through change and resolving conflicts in a diplomatic way.

They lead by example, setting high expectations and achieving them, so that people can see the great results and follow them because they trust their abilities.

They don't leave unfinished work because they don't want to see others seeing this bad habit as an example to be followed.

How Leaders Can Build Social Skills

1. *Improve their communication skills*
2. *Praise others for efforts*
3. *Learn conflict resolution*

The way leaders communicate with their teams can make a huge difference in performance. The more efficient and effective they communicate their messages, and the more they create strong relationships with others, the more likely they are to receive the desired feedback manifested through more powerful results.

It is also beneficial to praise your team or the members of your team who worked harder to achieve better results. It creates a sense of loyalty, self-esteem, and motivation.

In the end, leaders should have a solid understanding of how their emotions and actions affect the people around them.

Performance is achieved through people's power, but it's a long process that determines the level of productivity people manifest.

They have to be motivated, they have to receive concise indications, and they need to have a good relationship with their manager.

They need support and understanding. They need to be guided by someone who knows the process' steps and how they can be implemented, and they also need someone who can make them understand the vision of the entire work.

When people don't understand the desired outcome, they work chaotically.

Conclusion

Think about something: two managers are equally skilled, but only one of them is a team player.

Who will the boss hire or promote?

The answer is obvious: the one who's really good at leading people.

Employers don't seek only for professional expertise and experience in their employees, they are also looking for unique qualities such as character traits, interpersonal and communication skills that will help leaders motivate people, inspire and deliver a clear and enlightening vision.

You will be able to stand out and advance fast in your career if you have these traits.

Printed in Great Britain
by Amazon